WORLD OF INSECTS

Fireflies

by Emily K. Green

BELLWETHER MEDIA • MINNEAPOLIS, MN

Note to Librarians, Teachers, and Parents:

Blastoff! Readers are carefully developed by literacy experts and combine standards-based content with developmentally appropriate text.

Level 1 provides the most support through repetition of high-frequency words, light text, predictable sentence patterns, and strong visual support.

Level 2 offers early readers a bit more challenge through varied simple sentences, increased text load, and less repetition of high-frequency words.

Level 3 advances early-fluent readers toward fluency through increased text and concept load, less reliance on visuals, longer sentences, and more literary language.

Whichever book is right for your reader, Blastoff! Readers are the perfect books to build confidence and encourage a love of reading that will last a lifetime!

This edition first published in 2007 by Bellwether Media.

Library of Congress Cataloging-in-Publication Data
Green, Emily K., 1966–
    Fireflies / by Emily K. Green.
        p. cm. – (Blastoff! readers) (World of insects)
Summary: "Simple text accompanied by full-color photographs give an up-close look at fireflies."
    Includes bibliographical references and index.
    ISBN-10: 1-60014-013-0 (hardcover : alk. paper)
    ISBN-13: 978-1-60014-013-6 (hardcover : alk. paper)
    1. Fireflies–Juvenile literature. I. Title. II. Series.

QL596.L28G68 2006
595.76'44–dc22   2006002770

Table of Contents

4

Fireflies are **insects**. But fireflies are not flies. Fireflies are **beetles**.

Most fireflies are
black or brown.

Fireflies have flat bodies.

Most fireflies have red,
yellow, or orange marks.

A firefly has four wings.
Two hard wings in front
protect its body.

A firefly uses its back
wings to fly.

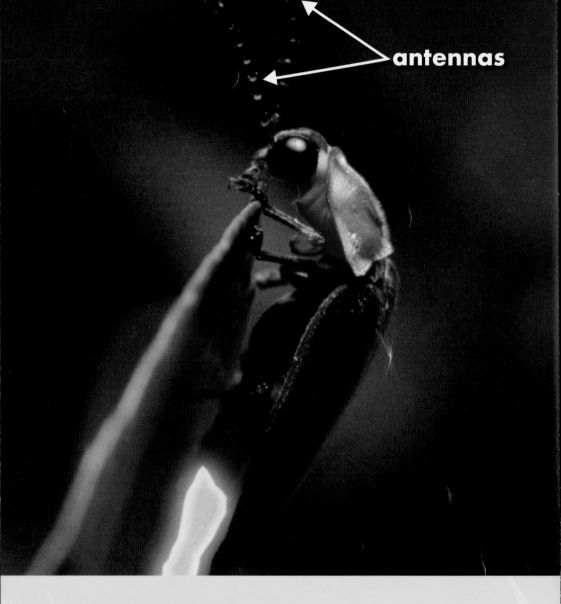

antennas

A firefly has two **antennas**. It uses its antennas to smell and feel.

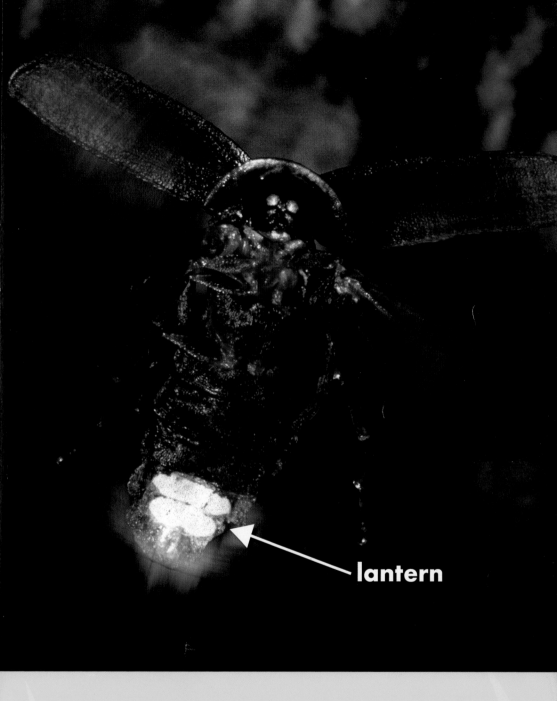

lantern

Some fireflies have **lanterns**. The lantern makes a glowing light.

Fireflies mix **chemicals** inside their bodies to make the light.

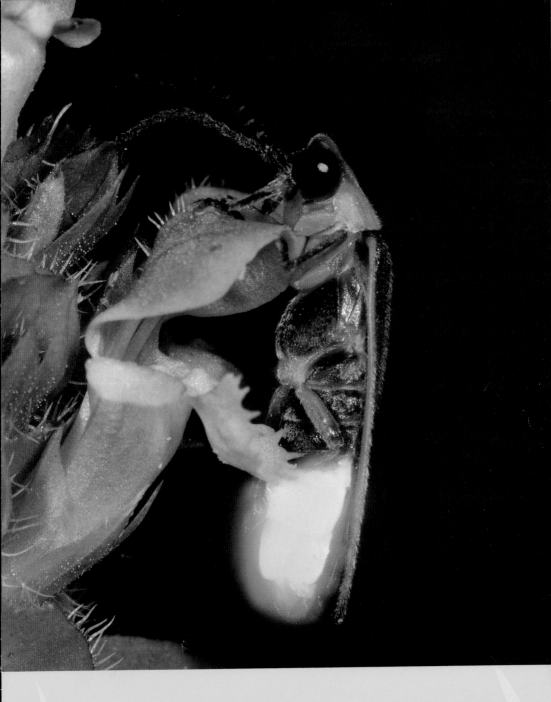

Blink. Blink. Fireflies can turn their lanterns on and off.

Fireflies flash their lanterns to find each other.

Male fireflies flash their lanterns at females while they fly.

Females blink back at males
from the ground.

Fireflies also flash their lanterns when they are in danger.

17

Fireflies rest on plants during the day.

Fireflies fly on summer nights.

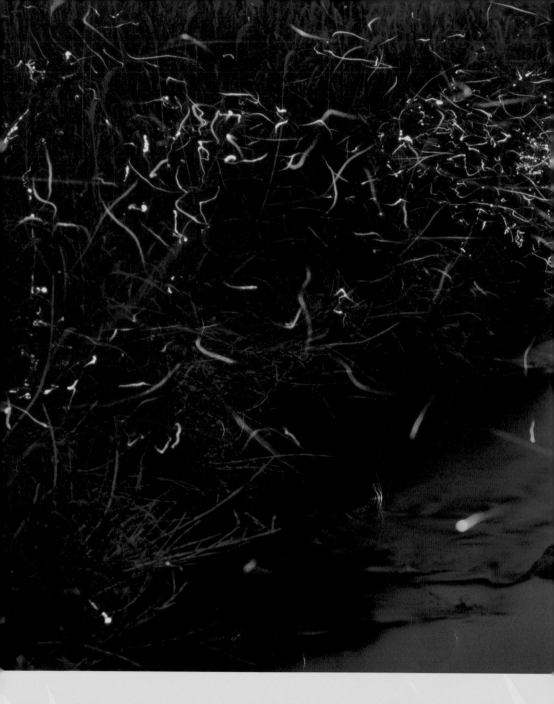

Fireflies glow brightly in the night. Some people call them lightning bugs.

Sometimes hundreds of fireflies flash their lanterns at the same time. Wow!

Glossary

antennas—the feelers on an insect's head; insects use the feelers to touch and smell things.

beetle—a kind of insect with a hard outer shell, six legs, and two sets of wings

chemicals—materials found in nature; sometimes mixing chemicals causes a reaction.

insect—a kind of animal that has a hard body; most insects also have two antennas, six legs, and two or four wings.

lantern—the part of a firefly's body that makes light; the light from a firefly's lantern never feels hot like a lightbulb.

To Learn More

AT THE LIBRARY

Brinckloe, Julie. *Fireflies*. New York: Macmillan, 1985.

Carle, Eric. *The Very Lonely Firefly*. New York: Philomel, 1995.

Drachman, Eric. *Leo the Lightning Bug*. Los Angeles: Kidwick Books, 2001.

Eastman, P.D. *Sam and the Firefly*. New York: Beginner Books, 1986.

Hawes, Judy. *Fireflies in the Night*. New York: HarperCollins, 1963.

Loewen, Nancy. *Living Lights: Fireflies in Your Backyard*. Minneapolis, Minn.: Picture Window Books, 2004.

Oppenheim, Shulamith Levey. *Fireflies for Nathan*. New York: Tambourine Books, 1994.

ON THE WEB
Learning more about fireflies is as easy as 1, 2, 3.

1. Go to www.factsurfer.com

2. Enter "fireflies" into search box.

3. Click the "Surf" button and you will see a list of related web sites.

With factsurfer.com, finding more information is just a click away.

Index

The photographs in this book are reproduced through the courtesy of: Kim Steele/Getty Images, front cover, p. 10; Dwight Kuhn Photography, pp. 4, 6, 8, 12, 13, 17; Varina Hinkle, p. 5; Danita Delimont/Alamy, p. 7; Phil Deginger/Alamy, p. 9; Maximillian Weinziel/Alamy, p. 11; Peter Arnold/Alamy, pp. 14-15; Bruce Colman/Alamy, p. 16; AM Corporation/Alamy, p. 18; B. Mete Uz/Alamy, p. 19; JTB Photo/Alamy, pp. 20-21.